The Library of
HOLIDAYS™

Martin Luther King Jr. Day

Leslie C. Kaplan

The Rosen Publishing Group's
PowerKids Press™
New York

To Elliot

Published in 2004 by The Rosen Publishing Group, Inc.
29 East 21st Street, New York, NY 10010

First Edition

Editor: Jannell Khu

Book Design: Michael J. Caroleo, Michael de Guzman, and Nick Sciacca

Photo Credits: Cover © AP/Wide World Photos; pp. 4, 8 © Flip Schulke/CORBIS; pp. 7, 11, 12, 15, 16 © Bettmann/CORBIS; pp. 19, 20 © CORBIS; p. 22 © Aneal Vohra/Index Stock Imagery, Inc.

Kaplan, Leslie C.
  Martin Luther King Jr. Day / Leslie C. Kaplan.—1st ed.
    p. cm.— (The library of holidays)
  Includes bibliographical references and index.
  Contents: What is Martin Luther King Jr. Day?—Unfair laws for black people—King's early years—Equal rights on the bus—Objecting peacefully—Lunchtime sit-ins—"I have a dream"—Reaching for the dream—Honoring King—Celebrating Martin Luther King Jr. Day.
  ISBN 0-8239-6661-5 (library binding)
  1. Martin Luther King, Jr., Day—Juvenile literature. 2. King, Martin Luther, Jr., 1929–1968—Juvenile literature.
  [1. Martin Luther King, Jr., Day. 2. Holidays. 3. King, Martin Luther, Jr., 1929–1968.] I. Title. II. Series.
  E185.97.K5K75 2004
  394.261—dc21

                                        2002009486

Manufactured in the United States of America

Contents

LBE 12/04 13.95

Martin Luther King Jr. Day

Reverend Martin Luther King Jr. was a leader of the American **Civil Rights movement**. Americans celebrate his birthday on the third Monday in January. They remember his dream that one day all men and women will live together in peace and equality, regardless of their skin color. They think about his belief that problems can be solved without **violence**. Many schools and businesses close for Martin Luther King Jr. Day. Parades, speeches, and church services are held to honor King's life and his ideas.

◄ *In the mid-1900s, Reverend Martin Luther King Jr. worked to gain equal rights for black people.*

Unfair Laws for Black People

Although black people were freed from **slavery** after the **Civil War**, they did not have the same rights as white people had. **Segregation** laws started in many states in the late 1800s. These laws kept blacks and whites apart. Black children went to schools that were **inferior** to the schools that white children attended. Blacks had to sit in the backs of buses. They could not vote in many towns. Blacks could not get well-paying jobs. Black people were treated poorly by white people, who disliked them for their skin color.

Segregation laws were especially practiced in the South. This photo was taken in 1947, in a segregated school in Virginia. ▶

Martin Luther King Jr. was born on January 15, 1929, in Atlanta, Georgia. When Martin was a young boy, the parents of a white boy stopped him from playing with Martin. It was because of Martin's skin color. Martin's parents explained to him that he was just as good as anyone else.

Martin studied hard in school. He attended college at age 15. Even at a young age, Martin wondered why there were unfair laws against blacks and thought of ways to change them.

◄ *Martin Luther King Jr. had deep religious feelings and chose to become a reverend, as had his father and grandfather before him.*

Objecting Peacefully

   Reverend King was a leader in the church and in the community. Black people wanted to end segregation. They went to King to ask for guidance. Reverend King did not believe in violence. His beliefs were based on those of a leader in India, Mohandas Gandhi. Both men believed in using peaceful means to work for change. King traveled to many cities in the United States to talk about equality for blacks. He told crowds of **demonstrators** that everyone has the right to fair **treatment** and that all people are born equal.

Reverend King arranged peaceful demonstrations to spread his ideas about justice. This prayer meeting was held in 1963. ▶

Equal Rights on the Bus

Alabama state law required blacks to sit in the backs of buses. Blacks also had to give up their seats to white people if the bus was full. In 1955, a black woman named Rosa Parks made history when she refused to give up her seat to a white man. When Parks was arrested, groups of black people went to King for advice. King told them to **boycott** the buses. For a year blacks walked, took taxis, or shared cars to get around. The bus company lost money. Finally in 1956, Alabama changed its unfair bus laws!

This photo of Parks sitting in the front of a bus was taken a year after she made history by breaking Alabama's unfair bus laws.

Lunchtime Sit-Ins

Young black people joined the movement to end segregation. In 1960, four black college students in North Carolina went to a restaurant and sat at the white people's lunch counter. This was illegal, and many white customers were angry about it. The students came back to the counter four days in a row. More students joined them. King led a march to support the students' efforts. News of the lunchtime sit-in spread throughout America. Black people in other southern cities started holding sit-ins at segregated lunch counters.

In 1960, black students held a sit-in at a counter that was reserved for white customers in Greensboro, North Carolina. ▶

"I Have a Dream"

In August 1963, Reverend King led a big civil rights march in Washington, D.C. More than 250,000 people of all races and backgrounds came together to support equality, peace, and freedom. King stood on the steps of the **Lincoln Memorial** and gave a speech. He said that he dreamed of a world in which all people lived together in peace. He said that he dreamed that someday black and white children would walk together as sisters and brothers. This famous speech is called "I Have a Dream."

◀ *Reverend King worked for most of his life to make his dream a reality. His dream was for all people to live together in peace.*

Reaching for the Dream

After the march to Washington, D.C., millions of people joined the Civil Rights movement. In 1964, the Civil Rights Act was passed. This act promised all Americans equal rights in education, housing, and voting. That same year, King was awarded the **Nobel Peace Prize**. However, some people disliked King's work to end segregation. Some of these people arrested or beat his followers. On April 4, 1968, somebody shot and killed Reverend King in Tennessee. Around the world, people were saddened by the news.

In front of government and civil rights leaders, President Lyndon B. Johnson signed the Civil Rights Act of 1964. ▶

Honoring King

Many people wanted to honor Reverend King with a national holiday. **Congress** said no for 15 years. Only George Washington and Christopher Columbus were honored with national holidays. King's wife, Coretta Scott King, and millions of others asked Congress to reconsider. Many states began celebrating Martin Luther King Jr. Day on January 15. Finally, in 1983, Congress voted to make Martin Luther King Jr. Day a nationwide holiday. President Ronald Reagan signed a bill to make the holiday official in 1986.

President Reagan signs a bill to make Martin Luther King Jr.'s birthday a national holiday. Coretta Scott King stands at the far left.

People of all races celebrate Martin Luther King Jr. Day. Students often spend the week before the holiday learning about King's life. You can put together a play with your classmates about King's life, or write an essay about how he has made the world a better place. You can see King's "I Have a Dream" speech on television. You can attend a church service that is held in King's honor. Some people march at night with candles. The lights are a reminder of how King's work has lit up the world.

Glossary

boycott (BOY-kot) To join with others in refusing to buy from or deal with a person, nation, or business.

civil rights movement (SIH-vul RYTS MOOV-mint) People and groups working together to win freedom and equality for all.

Civil War (SIH-vul WOR) The war fought between the Northern and Southern states of America from 1861 to 1865.

Congress (KON-gres) The part of the U.S. government that makes laws.

demonstrators (DEH-mun-stray-terz) People who take part in a march or a meeting to object or to make orders to bring about change.

inferior (in-FEER-ee-ur) Of poor quality or below average.

Lincoln Memorial (LEEN-kun meh-MOR-ee-ul) A monument that honors Abraham Lincoln, the sixteenth president of the United States.

Nobel Peace Prize (noh-BEL PEES PRYZ) An award of money given each year to a person or a group for working toward peace.

reverend (REV-rend) A church leader.

segregation (seh-gruh-GAY-shun) The act of keeping people of one race, gender, or social class apart from others.

slavery (SLAY-vuh-ree) The system of own person "owning" another.

treatment (TREET-ment) The act or manner of handling someone.

violence (VY-lens) Rough or harmful action.

23

Index

A
Alabama, 13
Atlanta, Georgia, 9

C
Civil Rights Act, 18
Civil Rights movement,
     5, 18
Civil War, 6
Congress, 21

G
Gandhi, Mohandas,
     10

I
"I Have a Dream,"
     17, 22

K
King, Coretta Scott,
     21

M
march, 14, 17–18

N
Nobel Peace Prize,
     18
North Carolina, 14

P
parades, 5
Parks, Rosa, 13

S
segregation, 6, 10,
     14, 18
sit-ins, 14
slavery, 6
speech(es), 5, 17,
     22

W
Washington, D.C.,
     17–18

Web Sites

Due to the changing nature of Internet links, PowerKids Press has developed an online list of Web sites related to the subject of this book. This site is updated regularly. Please use this link to access the list:
www.powerkidslinks.com/lhol/mlking/